a special gift...

for:

from:

date:

Enid —
    May every day be a beautiful
gift —
        Patricia Sheehy

Giving with Meaning

Turn ordinary items into meaningful gifts using folklore, legends and traditions

Patricia Sheehy

Oak Tree Press

Taylorville, IL

Oak Tree Press

Oak Tree Books may be purchased for educational, business, or sales promotional use. Contact Publisher for quantity discounts.

First Edition, June 2007

10 9 8 7 6 5 4 3 2 1

Cover and Interior Design by Mick Andreano, http://www.mickadesign.com/

The legends in this book have been gathered from stories and superstitions handed down through the ages. They are presented here for gift ideas and entertainment value only and are not to be taken literally. Neither the author nor publisher assume responsibility for their use or interpretation.

Library of Congress Cataloging-in-Publication Data

Sheehy, Patricia, 1946-
Giving with meaning : learn how to make every gift special : turn ordinary items into meaningful gifts using folklore, legends, and traditions / Patricia Sheehy.
p. cm.
ISBN-13: 978-1-892343-49-9 (alk. paper)
SBN-10: 1-892343-49-5 (alk. paper)
 1. Gifts. 2. Manners and customs. I. Title.
GT3040.S54 2007
394--dc22
                        2007007118

dedication

For my stepchildren Ann, Patty, Kathleen and Jimmy, who have been part of every gift-giving moment for over 30 years, bringing love, joy, and meaning to my life. And for my husband, Jim. If they handed out doctorates in gift-giving, he would definitely receive one.

acknowledgments

So many people have encouraged this project, believing in the power of thoughtful and creative gift-giving. In particular, I want to thank my good pal Gloria Amenta, who is kind and fun and has an eye for unique gifts, and Judy Robbins, a friend for all seasons, who knows how to give just the right present at just the right time, often "just because."

To Christy, Janice, Lisa, Karen and Chelsea — for as long as I can remember — and each in your own special way — you have showered me with thoughtful gifts and loving support, and I am forever grateful.

To Billie Johnson, my publisher, thanks for your gift of self. Every day, you take raw material and turn it into something beautiful. Deep appreciation also to Mick Andreano of Mickadesign.com for bringing this book to life through his artful layout and design.

I would also like to acknowledge the countless historians, storytellers and ordinary people who have passed down the legends and traditions that serve as the basis for this book.

How many times have your wracked your brain trying to come up with a small, thoughtful gift for the hostess of a dinner party? And what about Father's Day, birthday and graduation presents? Chances are you give at least fifteen gifts a year, not counting the holiday season, and chances are you've run out of steam when it comes to making creative, meaningful choices. This book will change all that.

Using folklore, legends and traditions, Giving with Meaning helps you transform ordinary items into extra-ordinary gifts. For instance, take that bottle of wine you always seem to give. Tie some tassels around it and suddenly it's more than a bottle of Chablis — it's a wish for good luck. Surprise your pregnant friend with a ceramic turtle and she'll be sure to have an easy delivery. Or buy that special someone a rose-colored sweater to declare your undying love.

The legends in this book have been gathered from stories and superstitions handed down through the ages. After each one, you will see suggested gift occasions. These are only suggestions — nearly all of the legends can be applied to any occasion. For example, gifts traditionally slated for the new year can be used for any new beginning or rite of passage, such as birthdays (the start of that person's new year), weddings, graduations, or job promotions.

The real secret to meaningful gift giving is creating a bridge between the gift, the person, and the occasion. Once you've decided on the legend you want to interpret, write out the story on a note card, either completely or paraphrased for your particular purpose, or use the gift tags provided at the back of the book. Then — here's the important part — add your own personal note linking all of the elements. Use the sample notes throughout the book or let them serve as inspiration for your own message. Whether handwritten or computer generated, your personal message, along with the legend, will make even the simplest gift seem unique and meaningful.

We all know that gift giving is here to stay. It's how we celebrate the important moments in our life — it's how we say get well ... congratulations ... I care ... I'm sorry. And, like it or not, what we choose to give, and how we present it, says as much about us as it does about the occasion and our relationship to the person receiving the gift. Giving with Meaning puts the spirit back into gift giving by making it fun, thoughtful and creative.

Enjoy the experience and make every day a meaningful one.

— PS

Acorn

Legend tells us that Thor — the god of storms — created thunder by flinging his hammer throughout the heavens whenever he was angry. The Norsemen believed that the mighty oak tree, which grows from a tiny acorn and is known as the tree of heaven, could protect them from Thor's rage. During a storm, they placed acorns on every windowsill in their home, thereby warding off all of the dangers associated with thunder and lightning.

Protector of the House

gift occasions

This is perfect for any type of hostess or housewarming gift. It also works well for wedding showers and birthdays. Try this for a new job or promotion gift to ward off the dangers of "corporate thunder and lightning."

gift ideas

- Crystal bowl or other container filled with real acorns, ready to be placed on window sills during storms
- Acorn ornaments, with ribbon for hanging at windows
- Stepping stone with acorn imprint for the garden or walkway
- A small oak tree
- Door wreath with pine cones (for health, wealth and power) and acorns (for protection)
- Anything made from the "mighty oak," from furniture to accessories
- Acorn window shade pulls or curtain tie-backs
- Curtains embroidered with acorns
- Brass acorn paperweight
- Acorn jewelry: tie bar, cuff links, earrings, necklace

add a note after the legend—

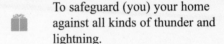 To safeguard (you) your home against all kinds of thunder and lightning.

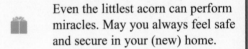 Even the littlest acorn can perform miracles. May you always feel safe and secure in your (new) home.

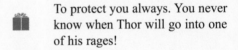 To protect you always. You never know when Thor will go into one of his rages!

I'm sorry I got angry. Use the acorn to remind me to talk softly and listen next time!

Bell

According to Irish tradition, a bell is used to maintain harmonious relationships by protecting against lover's quarrels. As soon as a disagreement begins, one of the lovers immediately rings the bell, breaking the spirit of discord and renewing the spirit of love.

Giving With Meaning

Keeper of Harmony

gift occasions

This is a couple's gift, ideally suited to a wedding, wedding shower, or anniversary. It also makes a nice hostess gift, instead of the "dinner" bell. Consider this for a retirement present, when the couple will suddenly find themselves together a whole lot more!

gift ideas

- A bell, made of anything from fine crystal to pottery or brass
- Wind chimes
- Jewelry or key ring with a bell-style charm attached
- Stuffed animal with a bell around its neck
- Door chimes or bell
- Clock with chimes
- Camp style bell or triangle
- Christmas bells for the door or a tree ornament
- CD of music featuring bells as an instrument
- Music box with bell-like sounds
- Zen-style garden bells or rain chimes

add a note after the legend—

May your life together always be filled with harmony and the spirit of love.

His and her bells: To ensure harmony in the togetherness of retirement.

To one of my favorite couples. You may never need this, but just in case. . .

Bird

According to Native American legend, birds have the power to carry our prayers directly to God. These prayers are carried on the feathers of a bird as he ascends toward the heavens with exceptional strength and speed. Because of this belief, Native Americans often bring feathers — either loose or in the shape of a fan — into church meetings.

Some spend an entire lifetime collecting the feathers of the most powerful birds — the bald eagle, the prairie falcon, the water turkey and the red-tailed hawk — in order to make a traditional twenty-four feather fan.

Conveyor of Prayer

gift occasions

This makes a wonderful gift of encouragement, recovery or get well. It's also ideal for any occasion when you want to offer up a prayer for happiness, health or success.

gift ideas

- Indian style jewelry or clothing that uses feathers as a motif
- Paper or silk fan where feathers are used in the design
- Bouquet of feathers, real or silk, tied with a beautiful bow or placed in a vase
- Beautiful robe or lounging outfit designed with feathers and/or birds
- Decorative arrangement made with feathers and/or artificial birds
- Bird house, bird bath or bird feeder
- Picture or photograph of birds in flight
- Canary, parakeet or other pet bird

add a note after the legend—

🎁 With prayers for your recovery — may they be carried from my lips to God's ears on the wings of a bird.

🎁 May all your prayers be answered, and may you know peace, happiness and health in the years ahead.

🎁 A gift of encouragement during this difficult time. Our prayers are with you.

Candles, Bread and Salt

According to Jewish tradition, a "threshold gift" of candles, bread and salt blesses the home of a friend or relative. These gifts symbolize the giver's prayer that the house will always be filled with light, bountiful food and spiced with joy.

A House Blessing

gift occasions

This is ideal for any type of hostess or housewarming gift. It also works well as a wedding or shower gift, as the couple will soon be setting up a new household. Don't forget to use this idea as a bon voyage gift for someone moving away.

gift ideas

Choose an interesting, funky or elegant container and create a gift basket that combines the elements of candles, bread and salt. Don't be afraid to be creative here. Here are a few ideas:

- Candles: special candles, candlesticks, oil lamps, aromatherapy candles

- Bread: loaf of specialty bread, gourmet breadsticks, cookbook, bread making machine, money (bread is slang for money)

- Salt: quartz crystal (salt of the earth) in the form of jewelry or a charm or simple stone, bath salts, kosher or sea salt, salt shaker, antique salt cellar

add a note after the legend—

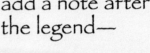 May your home always be blessed with good food, fine wine and the love of family and friends.

Wishing you continued joy and bounty. Thanks for a great evening.

As you set up your new home, may these gifts remind you of your many blessings.

Candles, Cake and Wine

Years ago, it was the Portuguese custom to have an "open house" from Christmas Eve until New Year's Day. During that time, every window in the house flickered with candlelight, a sign of welcome to all who passed by, strangers and friends alike. Each visitor was treated to a small cake and a cordial-sized glass of homemade wine.

A Welcoming Sign

gift occasions

Naturally, this custom translates into an ideal holiday gift. It also works well for hostess, housewarming, birthday and thank you gifts.

gift ideas

You can choose to give just the light/candle as a gift or an interesting combination of candles, cake and wine, presented in a gift bag or interesting container. Your combination basket could include any type of lighting or candles, a favorite cake and bottle of wine or a dessert wine. For an extra special gift, include wine glasses. Lighting ideas include:

- Single scented candle or an assortment of candles

- Crystal candlesticks or grouping of votive holders

- Small decorative lamp

- Electric or battery candles for lighting windows at holiday time

- Arrangement of pillar candles with flowers or greens

- Glass bowl with floating candles

add a note after the legend—

🎁 To someone who always makes me feel welcome. Thanks for your hospitality.

🎁 Thanks for always keeping a light in the window.

🎁 May your home always be filled with good friends and the soft glow of candlelight.

Carrots

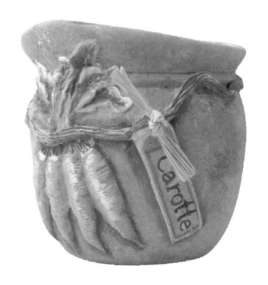

Carrots are considered a symbol of prosperity because the slices are coin-shaped and golden in color. The Hebrew word for carrots — *tsimes* — means to increase. In celebration of the new year, carrots are eaten with the hope of increasing goodness and happiness in the year ahead.

For Prosperity & Happiness

gift occasions

This is perfect for any "new beginning" occasion, from birthdays, weddings and job promotions, to religious and secular new year celebrations. It also works well as a housewarming gift or get-well wish.

gift ideas

- Carrot cake

- A favorite carrot recipe prepared and ready to eat, presented in a serving dish for your friend to keep

- Recipe box filled with a variety of carrot recipes

- Carrot seeds or plant

- China or pottery emblazoned with carrots

- Rabbit doll or stuffed animal, holding a carrot

- Don't forget Karat, as in diamond and other precious stones

add a note after the legend—

May your happiness double in the days ahead.

Here's hoping all your dreams come true. May every day of this "new year" bring you increased joy and fulfillment.

Wishing you a speedy recovery. May this mark the beginning of your renewed health.

The Cat

During the depression, hobos had a secret way of letting others know where they could find nourishment. They carved the face of a smiling cat on a fence post outside of homes where they had been fed. This meant a kind and generous person lived inside.

Symbol of Generosity

gift occasions

This is the perfect gift any time you want to honor a kind and generous person in your life. Consider Mother's or Father's Day, and birthdays. Makes a great hostess gift or thank you.

gift ideas

anything with cat motif, such as:

- Jewelry
- Notepad/stationery
- Cocktail napkins or guest towels
- Welcome Sign plaque
- T-shirt or hat
- Dessert plates

also:

- Decorative cat — ceramic, crystal, cloisonné
- Stuffed animal
- Real kitten (make sure it's appropriate and wanted!)
- Music or poster from the Broadway musical CATS
- Your own drawing/painting of a fence post with the face of a cat

add a note after the legend—

- Here's to another great dinner together. Thanks for your hospitality.
- You've always been there for me. This is my small way of saying thank you.
- For your kindness and generosity, thank you.

Cornucopia

The horn of plenty — spilling over with grains, vegetables and fruits — symbolizes a bountiful harvest. The horn is said to have been broken from the head of Amalthaea, the she-goat who nursed the god Zeus (Jupiter). In turning the horn into a cornucopia, Amalthaea promised Zeus that it would always be filled with the foods he loved. With that promise, Jupiter's image was set among the stars in the constellation known as Capricorn. In Roman times, a large sea shell was used as the horn; filled with fruit, it symbolized the abundance of life's material goods.

Symbol of Abundance

gift occasions

In addition to the classic Thanksgiving gift, this works well for any occasion, from a small hostess or housewarming gift to birthdays, showers, weddings, and retirement.

gift ideas

Fill any elegant or interesting container with a variety of "material goods." Look for containers in the shape of a cornucopia or seashell (a conch shell is the best choice). Here are some suggestions for filling with abundance:

- Selection of favorite candies, nuts, and fruit
- Collection of seashells and sea glass for display
- Coins or dollar bills and/or gift certificates
- Seashell charm on a necklace or bracelet
- Flowers or plant in a shell or cornucopia
- Edible fruit or cookie arrangement

Ideas for creating a theme-style cornucopia:

- All the makings for a special meal or dessert
- Selection of cheeses, crackers, and spreaders
- Favorite wine, along with wine accessories
- Soaps and bath/spa accessories
- Romantic music, candles, wine glasses & wine

add a note after the legend—

🎁 May your home (life) always be filled with abundance.

🎁 To celebrate the good things in life.

🎁 May your image be set among the stars and your life always filled with the best things life has to offer.

Egg

Because the egg symbolizes creation — the beginning of life and, therefore, the beginning of a new period of life — the Persians have a custom of giving one another eggs on New Year's Day. Chinese people present a red hard-boiled egg as symbol of congratulations when a baby is born. They also decorate a baby's layette with designs of eggs for luck and protection, as the egg's "eye" is said to watch over the child.

For Renewal and New Beginnings

gift occasions

In addition to a New Year's gift, this is perfect for any "new beginning" occasion, such as graduation, job promotion, or birthday. It also makes a wonderful baby gift.

gift ideas

- Basket of marble, cloisonné, or wooden colored eggs, or a single beautiful red egg

- Ukrainian egg, often decorated with symbols that recall prayer and worship

- Single collectible egg in a Faberge style; also consider crystal or hand-blown glass

- Gift certificate to brunch/breakfast

- Decorative bird's nest or bird house with eggs as part of the motif

- Daytrip to farmer's market for fresh eggs, followed by breakfast in a favorite restaurant

- Jewelry designed as a Faberge egg — easy to find around Easter

- Baby gifts, such as sheets, bumpers, blanket or wallpaper border, decorated with eggs, ducks and chicks

add a note after the legend—

Congratulations on your new beginning. Happiness always.

To mark this milestone in your life and all the new beginnings it represents.

For you and your new baby — wishing you all of life's best.

Evergreen

The rolling hills of Ireland are described as having forty shades of green. According to St. Patrick, green is the color of hope, representing the faith and optimism of the Irish people throughout history. The evergreen tree, which never looses its shape, color or leaves, has come to signify both hope and everlasting life.

For Eternal Hope

gift occasions

Obviously, this is perfect for any Irish person on your list, for any occasion. It's also an ideal way to express a wish for optimism, recovery, and long life. Consider get well, recovery, wedding, anniversary or birthday. Use this as a gift of encouragement for people struggling with cancer or another illness. Can also be used to express sympathy.

gift ideas

- Real, or silk, evergreen tree
- Gift certificate to a garden shop for an evergreen plant or tree
- Christmas greens tied with an extravagant ribbon or set in a decorative container
- Any plant that stays green year round
- Green-colored clothing or accessories for the home
- Green candle, for light and hope
- Painting of evergreen trees
- Green shawl, fleece blanket, or sweater (for warmth and recovery)
- Crystal candy dish filled with green jelly beans or spearmint leaves
- Glass paperweight with swirls of green
- Money (of the green variety)

add a note after the legend—

May your life together be evergreen and forever green. (play on words; perfect for money gift)

To the most optimistic person I know. Keep the faith and get well soon.

Like the fighting Irish, never give up hope.

Accept this evergreen tree as a symbol of my love and sympathy and the everlasting love you and your (husband, sister, father) shared.

Forget-me-not

According to German legend, a knight and his lady were walking along the banks of the Danube on the eve of their wedding when they saw a spray of beautiful blue flowers in the river below. She begged her lover to retrieve them for her. He dove into the water, clutching the flowers in his hand as the turbulent waters swept him away. Struggling against the current, the knight cried out, "forget me not." From that day forward, the lovely blue flowers had their name.

Symbol of Remembrance

gift occasions

This gift should be used primarily between sweethearts, although it can be adapted for special friends. Consider such events as wedding, anniversary, bon voyage and Valentine's Day.

gift ideas

- Forget-me-not plant or bouquet

- Forget-me-not seeds; include a planter and/or gardening tools

- Anything emblazoned with these lovely blue flowers. Look for enamel jewelry, silk scarves, handkerchiefs, note cards, mouse pads, china, or serving trays

- Painting or photograph of a garden filled with forget-me-not flowers

- Flowers pressed under glass

- Create a CD of "forget-me-not" love songs

- Write a poem or a love letter, listing the person's wonderful qualities and how you will love/remember them always

- A blank journal, with your inscription on the first page, about always remembering one another. Make this extra special by including an elegant pen

- Framed photo of you (and your special person), using forget-me-not flowers as a tie-on, or press a few beneath the glass

add a note after the legend—

A small token of my affection. Don't ever forget how much I care.

Like the knight, I'd go to great lengths to prove my love to you. Forget me not.

A small reminder of just how much I love you.

Wherever you go, no matter how much time passes, we'll be forever friends.

Garlic

Throughout history, garlic has been considered a natural healer, capable of improving strength and curing nearly every ailment. According to legend, Roman gladiators ate garlic to enhance their ability in the stadium. In ancient Egypt, garlic was so valuable as a remedy for headaches, throat disorders and physical weakness, it was actually used as currency: fifteen pounds of garlic would purchase a healthy male slave. Today, the legend continues — many people believe that garlic is more potent than penicillin in its ability to fight disease and boost the immune system.

For Healing and Strength

gift occasions

This is a classic well-wisher, perfect as a get well or recovery gift. It can also be used for birthdays and makes an ideal gift when you want to wish someone luck before undertaking a new challenge that might require strength or energy.

gift ideas

- Ceramic or terra cotta garlic roaster

- Garlic crusher

- Wooden salad bowl, garlic crusher, and ingredients and/or recipe for Caesar salad

- Garlic pills from the health food store

- Cookbook with recipes that use garlic as a main seasoning

- Book on garlic and its healing properties

- Gift certificate for authentic Italian or Mediterranean meal

- Pasta basket: may include pasta or pasta maker, bulbs of garlic, press, napkins and bowls

- Oils and vinegars infused with garlic; to make this extra-special, include a cruet set

add a note after the legend—

🎁 Use garlic every day to keep those pesky doctors away. Wishing you a speedy recovery.

🎁 Happy Birthday and many healthy years to come.

🎁 A touch of garlic, for power and prowess (strength, skill, energy) in tackling your latest challenge (list the challenge, such as running a race, accepting a new job, undergoing treatment).

Holly & Ivy

According to English legend, the holly plant is considered male and the ivy is known as the female. The first plant brought into the home by a visitor during the holiday season indicates which gender will rule the house in the coming year.

Ruler of the House

gift occasions

In addition to a holiday/new year gift, this works well as a hostess, wedding, anniversary, or promotion/new business gift any time of the year. Give as an encouragement gift to a newly-divorced friend, who is now in charge of his/her home.

gift ideas

A combination of holly and ivy makes the perfect "team" gift when both genders are involved: husband and wife, brother and sister, mother and father, male and female business partners. For single gender gifts, simply use the appropriate plant — holly or ivy — in your gift selection.

- Bottle of wine or champagne — tied with sprigs of holly and ivy, either silk or real

- Vase decorated with one, filled with sprigs of the other

- Basket or planter filled with one or both types of plants for indoor use. Make it extra special by including a watering can. Larger plants can be given for outside planting and an everlasting gift. Can also be combined with the Evergreen ideas (see separate listing)

- Nearly anything decorated with holly and ivy. Some ideas include: guest towels, soaps, throw pillows (get one for each), decorative china or pottery

- Paintings or photographs of one or both plants

- Paperweight or letter opener (ideal for new job gift)

add a note after the legend—

🎁 In celebration of your marriage, here is both holly and ivy. Wishing you a lifetime filled with love and teamwork.

🎁 Holly & Ivy, for two people who know how to make marriage work. Happy anniversary.

🎁 May you always rule the roost. Good luck.

🎁 Congratulations on your promotion. May you rule the office roost for many successful years.

Honey & Apples

Eating cakes made with honey, or pieces of apple dipped in honey, symbolizes the promise of a sweet year to come. This custom, now part of celebrating the Jewish New Year, has its origins with the harvest festivals of very early religions.

For a Sweet Year

gift occasions

This can be adapted to nearly any occasion, but works particularly well for the holiday season, as well as for birthday and hostess gifts. Try this for someone who has had a difficult time recovering from an illness.

gift ideas

- Cakes or breads baked or drizzled with honey; box of honey-glazed donuts
- Honey-baked ham
- Basket of apples and a jar of honey
- Honey pot
- Homemade apple pie and honey; give the pie in a decorative dish as part of the gift
- Honeycomb style candles
- "Pooh" bear or similar stuffed animal
- Candy jar filled with honey-flavored treats

add a note after the legend—

Every day is a new beginning. May the year ahead be filled with sweetness and love.

Wishing you all the sweetness and wonder life has to offer.

With each new day, may you find a new beginning, and may it be filled with sweetness.

Iron

A metal so strong it can be shaped only by fire, iron is known as the universal weapon against evil spirits, possessing both healing and protective powers. According to folklore, families can safeguard their homes by tacking a horseshoe over the door or placing a piece of iron at the threshold or under the bed. Believers "knock on iron" the ways others "knock on wood."

For Healing and Protection

gift occasions

This is perfect for housewarming and hostess gifts. It also works nicely for weddings, baby showers, or get-well wishes.

gift ideas

- Horseshoe
- Door knocker
- Wrought Iron lamp
- Candle holders
- Outside bench or other garden accessories/furniture
- Andirons or other fireplace accessories
- Old-fashioned tavern/iron puzzle
- Cast iron pots and pans
- Cast iron door stop in decorative styles and shapes
- Antique household items

on the lighter side:

- Iron-based vitamin pills (to help speed along recovery)
- Iron & ironing board (to keep away the evil spirits of wrinkles and scorches)

add a note after the legend—

🎁 To safeguard your home. May the angels smile on you always.

🎁 To keep you and yours safe and healthy in your new home — "knock on iron."

🎁 May your home always be a safe harbor, where love and happiness abound.

🎁 A small gift of healing and protection; may you always feel loved and safe.

Lettuce

Ever since Venus seduced her lover on a bed of lettuce, this leafy vegetable has been considered a powerful aphrodisiac. Further proof comes from Roman mythology, with stories about how Juno — the wife of Jupiter and protector of women and marriage — conceived a child after eating lettuce.

For Lovers Only

gift occasions

While this is an "anytime" gift between lovers, it would also be appropriate — and fun — as a wedding, wedding shower, or anniversary gift. Also fun for new parents who might need some time alone and a little "encouragement."

gift ideas

- Salad bowl and matching dishes

- Wooden salad bowl and Caesar Salad makings

- Gift basket with a variety of lettuces and salad dressings

- Cookbook specializing in salad and side dishes

- Gift certificate for a restaurant known for its salad bar

- Homemade dinner for the couple, delivered with a huge green salad and bottle of wine

- If you want to give a money gift, try this idea: crimp dollar bills and tie each in the center and place them in a glass salad bowl so that these "greens" have the feeling of lettuce

- Mood-setting extras: Any of these gifts could be accompanied by candles or a CD of romantic music, or babysitting services if the couple has children

add a note after the legend—

For those times when the spirit's willing but the body needs a little help!

Enjoy. Put Venus to shame!

A little seduction for the newlyweds (or for the happily married couple, or the new parents). Enjoy every moment of your lettuce-induced evening.

For a couple who shows others what love is all about. Just add lettuce and enjoy. (use this when you give accessories but not lettuce)

Lover's Knot

Throughout the world, the tying of knots symbolizes love, loyalty and friendship. According to European folklore, a woman could retain her lover's interest by tying a knot in his handkerchief and placing it in his breast pocket. Bridal bouquets often have cascading ribbons in which many knots have been tied, each one holding wishes for fidelity and happiness.

For Love and Loyalty

gift occasions

This sweetheart's gift can also be used to acknowledge special friendships. It makes the perfect going away present, as well as anniversary, wedding, shower, birthday or Valentine's Day gifts.

gift ideas

- Handkerchief, tie or scarf — be sure to tie a knot for presentation purposes
- Love-knot jewelry, such as earrings, ring or tie-tac
- Long strand of beads or pearls that can be knotted
- Sweater with decorative knots
- Chenille or fleece throw with knotted fringe
- Hair ribbons
- Rope hammock

add a note after the legend—

- To remind you always of how much I care.
- Wherever you are, we'll always be friends. Forget me knot.
- Wishing you a lifetime of love, loyalty, and happiness as you begin married life.
- I'll miss you while you're away (trip, college, military). Whenever you use/wear this, remember our special bond.

Metals

Ancient Egyptians adorned themselves with bright pieces of metal — the brighter and shinier the better — as protection against harm and evil spirits. Even today, this custom is observed by Egyptian women, who wear glittery ornaments in their hair or around their neck in order to ward off evil influences.

Protection from Harm

gift occasions

Because you're offering protection with this gift, it's ideal for any rite of passage, such as graduation, retirement or leaving home. This also works well as a birthday or get-well gift.

gift ideas

- Clothing studded with rhinestones or other glittery decorations

- Barrettes, combs, or other hair ornaments

- Jewelry made of metal, such as copper or brass. Museum stores and catalogs often have items with an Egyptian design

- Key ring or money clip

- Hat pin with glittery head. These are often worn on lapels as well as hats

- Angel jewelry in a shiny metal

add a note after the legend—

- A bit of precious metal to keep you safe from harm as you travel new and exciting paths.

- A touch of (copper, brass, etc.) to keep you safe and well.

- Angelic Metal — what better guardian to keep you safe every single day?

Money & More

Legend tells us that in the North of England when babies are taken out of the house for the first time, they are given four things: money, salt, a piece of bread, and an egg. This custom ensures that the child will never want for the necessities of life.

For Life's Necessities

gift occasions

This is the perfect birth, adoption or christening gift. It is also ideal for any rite of passage where the person is leaving home or starting over. Consider graduation, going off to college, wedding, bon voyage, or retirement. It also makes an interesting and supportive gift for a newly divorced person in need of encouragement.

gift ideas

Any creative combination of the four elements — money, salt, bread, egg — in an interesting basket, container, or tote bag:

- Money: silver dollar, "piggy" bank with money, roll of quarters, savings bond, gift certificate, stocks & bonds. You could also purchase coins commemorating the person's birth date. Here's another idea: take a stack of new dollar bills to a "quick" printer and have them bound on one side like a pad (teenagers love this!).

- Salt: sea or kosher salt, salt shakers or cellars, bath salts, quartz crystal (salt of the earth) jewelry

- Bread: a special loaf of bread, muffins, donuts, bread basket, cookbook, bread maker.

- Egg: "collectible" egg, jewelry designed as a Faberge egg, bed sheets or clothing decorated with eggs, Easter basket, certificate for breakfast, omelet recipes, egg timer, or soft boiled egg dishes. Fill a hollow Easter egg with money or a small treasure.

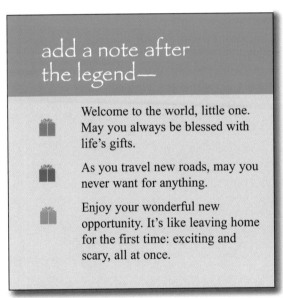

add a note after the legend—

Welcome to the world, little one. May you always be blessed with life's gifts.

As you travel new roads, may you never want for anything.

Enjoy your wonderful new opportunity. It's like leaving home for the first time: exciting and scary, all at once.

Mustard Seed

Faith as tiny as a mustard seed can move a mountain. — (Matthew 17:20)

From ancient times, the mustard seed has been used as a talisman for hope and faith in the future, often given to others as a prayer of encouragement.

Symbol of Hope

gift occasions

This is particularly nice for any occasion that calls for a little encouragement — recovery or get-well, graduation, leaving home, or simply *I know you can do it*. It's also a nice way to thank someone for having faith in you or helping you through a crisis.

gift ideas

- Jewelry encasing an actual mustard seed. Often seen in charms and pendants. Look for vintage pieces

- Jar of gourmet, whole-grained mustard

- Basket filled with small jars of mustard. Can also include sausages, cheese and crackers

- Certificate to lunch at a deli "where mustard graces every sandwich"

- Mustard plant or package of seeds and gardening tools or planter

- Bookmarks or prints with faith-based/mustard seed sayings

add a note after the legend—

🎁 Wishing you a brighter tomorrow. Keep the faith.

🎁 Keep hope alive and you'll find dreams do come true.

🎁 Thanks for all your support. Like the mustard seed, you've given me the faith to believe in myself (my dreams).

Oriental Noodles

Historians tell us that Chinese people were eating wheat noodles as early as 100 B.C. and that China is regarded as the birthplace of pasta. Because noodles have remained an integral part of Asian culture throughout the centuries, they are considered a symbol of longevity. It's considered bad luck to cut them. Noodles are traditionally served at birthdays and weddings with wishes for a long, happy life.

Symbol of Longevity

gift occasions

Following Asian tradition, use noodles for birthday and wedding wishes. Because this is well suited for any time you want to wish someone a long, joy-filled life, it works for nearly any situation. Consider get-well, retirement, and hostess gifts.

gift ideas

- Basket of noodles from various cultures, in differing shapes and colors
- Theme/ethnic dinner basket, with noodles and sauces from a particular culture
- Pasta or Oriental noodle cookbook
- Pasta maker
- Gift certificate to an Asian restaurant
- Pot of home-made chicken noodle soup (or any other noodle-based soup)

on the lighter side

- for poolside fun: noodles in various colors

add a note after the legend—

🎁 May your life together be long and healthy and filled with joy.

🎁 With wishes for a speedy recovery and a long, healthy life.

🎁 The best is yet to come. Have fun on your birthday and may you be blessed with the gift of longevity.

Peach Blossom

The Chinese believe that peach blossoms have the power to ward off illness and danger. They embrace this belief by hanging branches of peach blossom on the outside of their homes, thereby preventing guests from bringing in any unwanted influences.

Guardian of the Home

gift occasions

This makes a great hostess or housewarming gift. Also works well for birthdays, wedding showers or a token of friendship.

gift ideas

- Branches of real or silk peach blossoms
- Small peach tree, delivered and planted
- Peach blossom potpourri
- Basket of ripe peaches
- Peach preserves
- Peach-colored bath or guest towels
- Mailbox or welcome sign painted with peach blossoms

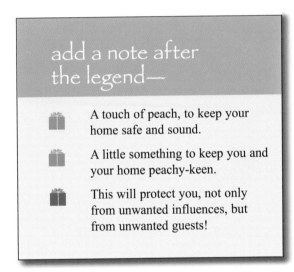

add a note after the legend—

🎁 A touch of peach, to keep your home safe and sound.

🎁 A little something to keep you and your home peachy-keen.

🎁 This will protect you, not only from unwanted influences, but from unwanted guests!

Periwinkle Plant

According to folklore, periwinkle should be planted in the garden of a couple's first home. This will ensure a long and happy life together, as the flower symbolizes "happy recollections."

For Happy Memories

gift occasions

This should be reserved for wedding, wedding shower, anniversary, and housewarming gifts.

gift ideas

- Periwinkle plant or seeds, along with planter or gardening tools
- Framed photograph or painting of periwinkles
- Arrangement of pressed flowers under glass
- Planter, trivet or mugs with periwinkles
- Guest towels embroidered with periwinkles
- Gift certificate to garden store
- Photo album, scrapbook, or memory box for storing sentimental objects, emblazoned with periwinkles

add a note after the legend—

- May you build a wealth of happy memories in your new home.

- Wishing you periwinkle days and star-studded nights. Happiness always.

- Here's to creating a lifetime of joy-filled memories.

Pig

In Germany, a person's good luck is acknowledged with the phrase "you have had pig." This custom dates back to times when food and money were scarce and having a pig to eat was a sign of extreme good fortune. Today, the pig is considered a good luck charm, much like the four-leaf clover or rabbit's foot.

Giving With Meaning

Symbol of Good Fortune

gift occasions

Because you can use this to wish someone good luck or to celebrate their good fortune, it's a very versatile, all-occasion gift idea. It can be used for someone going off on their own, entering a new phase of life or having difficulty. You can also use this to acknowledge graduation, job promotion, or some special achievement.

gift ideas

- Anything made of pig skin, such as a belt, wallet, gloves or jacket
- Piggy bank — add some coins for extra luck
- Honey-baked ham
- Home-made ham or pork chop dinner, delivered to the person's door, complete with candles, napkins and dessert.
- Picnic basket with ham sandwiches and all the fixings for a picnic
- Collectible pig in ceramic, crystal or wood
- Anything with a pig motif, such as jewelry, coffee mugs or pencil holder

add a note after the legend—

- When fortune comes your way, you'll know it's because you've had pig! Wishing you much luck and happiness in your new venture.

- Happy Birthday. Wishing you luck and good fortune in the coming year.

- Congratulations on your achievement — wishing you lots of luck in the days ahead.

Pineapple

The pineapple became a symbol of hospitality during Colonial times when seafaring was a way of life for many settlers. Whenever a New England sea captain returned from a voyage to the South Seas, he would bring back a pineapple and spear it on the gate outside his home. This was his way of announcing that he had returned and friends were welcome to call.

For Hospitality & Friendship

gift occasions

This is the perfect gift for a close friend on nearly any occasion. It's also an ideal wedding, hostess, or housewarming present.

gift ideas

- Basket of fresh pineapples — include a pineapple corer, a small knife and specialty napkins for a "ready-to-use" gift

- Recipes for pineapple-based foods

- Anything for the house with a pineapple motif. Ideas include: door knocker, napkin ring, salt & pepper shakers, paper weight, letter opener

- Jewelry in the shape of a pineapple, such as earrings, pin, or cuff links

- Windsock or flag with a pineapple design

- Welcome sign

- On the extravagant side: trip to Hawaii or a South Sea island

add a note after the legend—

For the perfect host and hostess. Thanks for your wonderful hospitality.

To friendship. And to you, my very special friend.

A symbol of hospitality for someone who always makes others feel right at home.

A symbol of our friendship. It means more than words can say.

Rainbows & Irises

According to American Indian legend: one autumn day, the Great Spirit overheard a conversation between all of the flowers in the meadow. Winter was coming and they would soon have to leave, but they wished they could continue sharing their magnificent colors with the earth. After much thought, Great Spirit granted their wish by giving them the sky as their heavenly landscape. Whenever we see a rainbow, we are looking at a display of flowers from the past.

In Greek mythology, Iris is the goddess of the rainbow, which is said to be an omen of great joy, foretelling happiness and abundance. It is also viewed as a symbolic bridge between heaven and earth, representing truth and regeneration.

For Truth, Hope & Joy

gift occasions

This works well for nearly any gift-giving occasion. Try this for a birthday or graduation gift or for Mother's Day. It makes a nice friendship or get-well gift. As an expression of sympathy, it provides comfort by offering a symbolic link between heaven and earth.

gift ideas

- Anything in the shape of a rainbow or iris
- Opal stone, said to contain all the colors of the rainbow
- Sun catcher or prism or anything made of crystal that catches light
- Kaleidoscope
- Box of crayons, perhaps in a collector-type tin
- Colorful candy
- Bouquet of Irises or bulbs for planting
- Hand-painted plate or serving dish
- Framed painting or photograph of a rainbow

add a note after the legend—

- May these colors touch your soul and bring you happiness in the days ahead.
- (Name of person who has died) will always be with us. We are all part of God's plan and only a rainbow away from those who have passed over.
- Congratulations on your achievement. May you experience the beauty of the rainbow every day.
- My dear friend, this iris (or rainbow) represents my wish for your enduring happiness. May you always know truth and joy and feel connected to both the visible and invisible.

Rose

According to mythology, Venus was carrying a vial of precious nectar as she hurried off to see her lover Adonis. Thinking only of their meeting, she carelessly stepped on a thorn, and punctured her foot. Blood from the wound stained the thorny bush. Nectar spilled upon its leaves. It's said that where the blood and nectar mingled, a magnificent red rose appeared. Since that time, the rose has symbolized both love and beauty.

Symbol of Love & Beauty

gift occasions

This is a gift for all those times you want to express sentiments of love and appreciation of beauty. In particular, consider the rose for wedding, anniversary, graduation and birthday gifts, as well as Valentine's Day and Mother's Day.

gift ideas

- Roses — a single one, a bouquet, or a rose bush for planting
- Rose potpourri or rose petals and container
- Rose-colored glass/crystal
- Kaleidoscope with rose petals or rose colored stones
- Rose-colored scarf or sweater
- Rose-colored jewelry, such as rose quartz
- Jewelry or charms in the shape of a rose
- Anything with pressed roses, such as jewelry box or photo album
- CD with songs such as "Roses & Lollipops," "Theme from The Rose" or "La Vie En Rose"

add a note after the legend—

Wishing you a life (birthday, new year) filled with the promise of the rose. May you always know beauty, joy and love.

The beauty of the rose pales next to the beauty you bring to my life. I love you.

Rose-colored and given in love. To remind you always of how much I care.

Rosemary

Because rosemary is said to ensure faithfulness, a bride often uses sprigs of this herb in her bouquet or hair wreath, as well as in the groom's boutonniere. In ancient times, the bride presented each guest with a branch of rosemary, tied with silken ribbons, as a symbol of love and loyalty. After the ceremony, tradition calls for the bride to plant the sprigs from her bouquet in the garden of her new home for her future daughters to use.

For Faithfulness

gift occasions

This symbol of fidelity is the perfect gift for wedding, wedding shower, anniversary, engagement or commitment of love. Combine it with the lover's knot for added meaning.

gift ideas

- Rosemary plant or seeds to plant in the garden

- Wreath made with sprigs of rosemary, ribbons and lover's knots. Combine it with other elements, such as evergreen, and rose-colored ribbon and write out a card explaining the meaning of each item

- Sprigs of rosemary (silk or real) tied to a bottle of champagne or other gift

- Scarf or handkerchief embroidered with rosemary

- Coasters or china plates emblazoned with painting of rosemary

- Decorative spice container filled with rosemary

- Kitchen towels embroidered with various herbs, including rosemary

add a note after the legend—

🎁 To celebrate your wonderful love. A bit of rosemary to carry out the custom.

🎁 A touch of rosemary, to remind you of the day you said "I do." Happy Anniversary.

🎁 A pledge of my fidelity, now and forever.

Salt

A Roman king asked his three daughters to describe their love for him. The oldest daughter said she loved her father as much as bread; the middle one said as much as wine. The youngest daughter said she loved her father as much as salt. Offended at being compared to such a common substance, the king banished this third daughter from his presence. One day, desperate to show her father just how precious her comparison had been, she had her father served a completely saltless meal. Realizing how bland life is without salt, he recognized the depth of her love and welcomed her back into his life.

Because of its lasting quality, salt is strongly associated with friendship and trust. Gypsies traditionally use bread and salt to confirm an oath. In Eastern countries, salt is placed before strangers as a pledge of good will. Salt is also considered one of the best amulets for warding off evil. In 17th century Europe, Inquisitors wore bags of salt as protection against the witches they sent to the gallows. Even today, superstitious people sprinkle salt over the threshold of a new house to prevent the entry of evil spirits.

Friendship, Trust & Protection

gift occasions

Use this to proclaim love, trust, friendship or protection from harm. It's a must for Father's Day. Other ideal occasions include housewarming, hostess and going away gifts.

gift ideas

- Basket of various salts, such as kosher and sea salt
- Saltwater taffy
- Bath salts
- Anything made of quartz crystal (salt of the earth); look for jewelry, paperweight, collective animals and other items
- Salt shaker
- Antique salt cellars
- Salted crackers with gourmet spread

add a note after the legend—

🎁 You're the salt of the earth. I love you. Happy Father's Day.

🎁 To ensure that only good spirits — those of happiness, love and health — cross the threshold of your new home.

🎁 Some people seal friendship with a kiss. Ours is also sealed with salt. (Good luck; I'll miss you; Hurry back).

Sun and Moon

Years ago, physicians prescribed gold as a tonic to help strengthen the heart. Silver was used for depression and memory failure. Today, the sun, which is golden colored, is known as the ruler of the heart, while the moon, which is silver, rules the head.

Ruler of Heart & Head

gift occasions

This is an all-occasion gift that works particularly well for birthday, anniversary, friendship, romance, get well, and new beginnings, such as graduation, new job, and moving away. Also, try giving this at the beginning of a new relationship.

gift ideas

You can choose nearly anything in gold or silver, or find items with depictions of the sun and moon, which represent heart and head. Combine the two, or use them separately, depending upon your intentions. Wrap your gift in one color paper and use the other for a ribbon when you want to depict both gold and silver.

- Jewelry in either gold or silver, or a combination of both. Consider pairs, such as earrings, charms, or cuff links, one in the shape of the sun, the other, the moon

- Gold and silver pencils

- Tray or basket emblazoned with the sun, filled with moon-shaped cookies

- Sun and/or moon dial

- Yellow flowers (roses, gladiola, sunflowers, etc) in a silver-colored vase

- Floating candles in the shape of suns and moons

- Brass candlesticks with silver-colored candles

- Grandfather clock with sun and moon phaser

- Gold and silver-toned flatware

- China in a pattern that uses either gold or silver, or both

add a note after the legend—

🎁 For the yin and yang of life: May your life always be ruled by both heart and head.

🎁 Gold, to help me find a place in your heart. Silver, so you'll never forget me.

🎁 A touch of gold and silver. Hope you recover your balance real soon.

🎁 A bit of silver, to celebrate your clear-headed thinking. Good luck with the promotion.

🎁 A bit of gold to help you follow your heart. Good luck.

Tassels and Fringe

According to legend, tassels and fringes ensure a blissful life. In ancient Europe, amulets of tassels were worn to guarantee happiness, and in Mexico they are still considered a symbol of good luck. In the Middle East, it's believed that evil spirits will go to great lengths to avoid anything with either tassels or fringe.

For Luck & Happiness

gift occasions

This can be used whenever you want to extend a wish for luck and happiness. Consider baby or birthday gifts, as well as graduation, retirement, bon-voyage, hostess or housewarming.

gift ideas

- Vest, sweater, or any piece of clothing with tassels or fringe

- Boots or moccasins with fringe

- Jewelry with a tassel effect

- Tie backs for curtains

- Pillow with tassels or fringe

- Fringed blanket, bed-spread or cotton throw

- Beaded tassel to hang in a window, from a curtain rod, or on a Christmas tree; look for these during the holiday season, often created as ornaments

- Tie a tassel or a piece of fringe to any gift or make it part of the wrapping and include a short note with your special wishes

add a note after the legend—

- Wear this whenever you need a little extra luck in your day.

- For added bliss. Wishing you a lifetime of happiness.

- A little tassel for lots of happiness and good luck.

Tea Time

The first cup of tea moistens my lips and throat, the second shatters my loneliness, the third causes the wrongs of life to fade gently from my recollection, and the fourth purifies my soul, while the fifth lifts me to the realm of the unwinking gods. — Chinese mystic/Tang Dynasty, 619-905

Serving tea is a time-honored symbol of friendship. The Chinese ceremonial tea was established as a time to set aside conflicts and come to peace with one's self, as well as with one another.

Symbol of Peace & Friendship

gift occasions

This works for any occasion that also celebrates friendship, including birthday, wedding, hostess and thank you gifts. It's ideal for get-well and recovery gifts, where the person needs some inner peace and, of course, for making up after an argument.

gift ideas

- Selection of teas and tea biscuits
- Basket filled with tea/mug/tea infuser
- China teacup and saucer
- Silver tea service or china teapot
- Teapot or kettle
- Miniature collector's tea set
- Certificate for High Tea
- Book on preparing and serving tea
- Tea cozy
- One of the nicest gifts might simply be inviting your friend over for a cup of tea and a long visit, or bringing all the makings to his or her house. As a remembrance of the afternoon, make sure to give your friend a small token gift of tea or a tea cup.

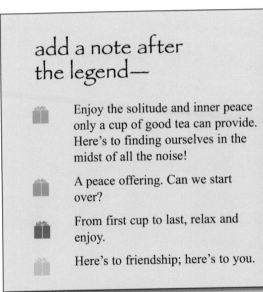

add a note after the legend—

Enjoy the solitude and inner peace only a cup of good tea can provide. Here's to finding ourselves in the midst of all the noise!

A peace offering. Can we start over?

From first cup to last, relax and enjoy.

Here's to friendship; here's to you.

Thyme

In the Middle Ages, when a knight left for the Crusades, his lady would present him with sprigs of thyme. This special herb means "loving remembrance" and a scarf embroidered with a design of thyme was a favored farewell gift. Legend also tells us that the French Republics considered thyme a symbol of bravery. They used the herb to summon loyalists to clandestine meetings — a sprig delivered to the door signified a secret meeting.

For Bravery & Remembrance

gift occasions

This is perfect for any farewell occasion, from a business or pleasure trip to moving away or going off to college. This can be used for the person leaving, or the one being left behind. It's also a nice "long distance" birthday or holiday gift and an excellent way to express sympathy. Use this to offer support and encourage bravery during difficult times. You could also summon your lover to a clandestine meeting with a bottle of wine decorated with sprigs of thyme delivered to his or her door by messenger.

gift ideas

- Scarf or handkerchief embroidered with design of thyme

- Notebook or journal with thyme on the cover

- Sprigs of thyme tied with knotted ribbons (see lover's knots)

- Bottle of champagne, wine, or special scent (perfume or cologne) decorated with ribbons and sprigs of thyme

- Picnic basket filled with "romantic" items — sprigs of thyme, wine, bread, music — and an invitation to meet at a certain time and place

- Thyme plant for the garden or kitchen

- Spice jar decorated or filled with thyme

add a note after the legend—

- Wherever you go, carry my love with you.

- To my dear friend — in loving remembrance of all the good times.

- Thyme is on your side: wishing you courage during this latest challenge.

- In loving remembrance of (name of person). (She/he) will always be with us, in spirit and in the wonderful memories we carry. My deepest sympathy.

Tomato

Throughout Italy, the tomato is considered a symbol of good fortune. Tomato sauce — simmering away on the stove — is said to bring health and wealth into the home. To further ensure prosperity, Italians often place a large red tomato on the mantle.

For Health & Wealth

gift occasions

This is a classic all-occasion gift, when "well-wishing" is called for. Consider get-well, housewarming, birthday, retirement and wedding shower as a few of the best occasions. Don't forget Mother's and Father's Day.

gift ideas

- Basket of plum or native tomatoes
- Basket filled with the makings of a spaghetti dinner
- Spaghetti pot
- Kitchen towels emblazoned with tomatoes
- Cookbook with pizza, pasta and tomato recipes
- Tomato plant or seeds
- Gift certificate to Italian restaurant
- Tomato-shaped salt and pepper shakers
- Ceramic, porcelain or crystal tomato for the mantel
- Homemade pasta dinner, your place or theirs
- Pizza delivery along with a card or note

add a note after the legend—

- Wishing you health, happiness and much prosperity.
- A wish for your speedy recovery. May you grow stronger and healthier every day.
- May your home always be filled with the wealth of good friends and the peace of good health.

Turtle

According to Chinese and Indian folklore, turtles embody the earth's energy — they are a symbol of patience, good health and long life. They are said to have curative powers and will ensure that pregnant women have an easy pregnancy and delivery. By the way, it is considered bad luck to own a turtle and then give it away.

For Health & Easy Pregnancies

gift occasions

Be sure to include this as part of any shower gift for the mother-to-be. As a wish for longevity and good health, it also makes a wonderful get-well, birthday, or thinking-of-you gift.

gift ideas

- Turtle jewelry — pins, bracelets, earrings, tie-tac
- T-shirt, night shirt, or other clothing emblazoned with turtles
- Pictures or posters of turtles
- Membership to an aquarium for turtle-viewing anytime
- Real pet turtle (only if you know it will be cared for)
- Collectible turtle: stuffed, crystal, wooden or china
- Turtle candy (chocolate and caramel available almost anywhere)

add a note after the legend—

Wishing you a long and joyous life filled with peace, patience, and good health.

With sincere wishes for your speedy recovery. May this turtle help you through your difficult time.

Hope the legend is true — keep this turtle close by for an easy pregnancy and pain-free delivery.

Wedding Basket

In traditional Navajo weddings, a special ceremonial basket is used to represent the union of two people destined to be together. Made of interwoven coils, the "braided" basket is said to symbolize the joining of soul mates — of spirits forever linked — in this world and the next, for all eternity.

Destiny Fulfilled

gift occasions

This special idea should be reserved for a wedding, wedding shower, anniversary or Valentine's Day gift.

gift ideas

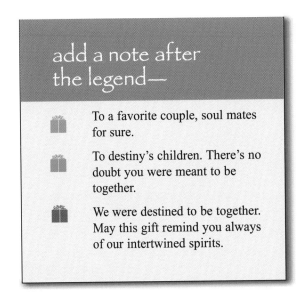

- Elegantly crafted basket, perhaps filled with other symbolic gifts

- Hand-crafted bowl or vase with a coiled or interwoven effect

- Braided rug, place mats or coasters

- Jewelry designed to suggest interwoven coils, such as a rope necklace or bracelet or wedding bands designed with a braided effect

- Anything special or elegant that suggests a braided or linking effect

add a note after the legend—

To a favorite couple, soul mates for sure.

To destiny's children. There's no doubt you were meant to be together.

We were destined to be together. May this gift remind you always of our intertwined spirits.

Wheat

Throughout history, wheat has symbolized an abundant harvest and used as a wish for fruitfulness. In Rome, wedding cakes were made of plain wheat. After the bride and groom tasted the first piece, the rest of the cake was crumbled over the head of the bride to ensure a bountiful life.

Symbol of Abundance

gift occasions

If you use the entire legend, it is best suited to wedding, wedding shower and anniversary gifts. However, if you simply use the first line and then add your own personal note, it can be used for nearly any occasion. Consider hostess, birthday, or job promotion gifts. Makes an interesting Mother's or Father's Day gift.

gift ideas

- Cake, muffins or bread made of wheat
- Cereal bowls and box of cereal
- Dried (or silk) shafts of wheat tied with beautiful ribbons and placed in a vase
- Plaque, welcome sign or door mat decorated with wheat shaft
- Cookbook that deals primarily with baking
- Wheat germ in a decorative container
- Fill a cornucopia or large shell with wheat products (see cornucopia legend)
- Extra special: trip to the mid-west to see the wheat fields

add a note after the legend—

To a wonderful couple. May God bless your marriage and grace you with life's bounty.

In celebration of your abundant harvest. Congratulations on your promotion.

Thanks for sharing your harvest with us. Dinner is always a special time at your home.

Mom (Dad), thanks for the richest bounty of all: your time and your love.

White Gifts

The custom of "white gifts" was first used by a Methodist Church in 1904 and is still observed around the world. It is based upon a legend that tells about celebrating the birth of Christ with gifts of love. Rather than material gifts, these are gifts of self, service and substance. Individuals are encouraged to write down personal commitments, which could be anything from a promise to break a habit or change an attitude, to promises of personal service.

Of Self & Service

gift occasions

This is a nice way to celebrate the holidays, as well as religious rites of passage. Also consider birthdays, anniversaries and even sympathy. Gifts of service are wonderful for parents and elderly people, who don't need things but might need company or help with chores. This also presents an opportunity to change negative ways and attitudes.

gift ideas

- Gift certificate for services, such as running errands, house-sitting, baby-sitting or lawn mowing. Don't forget more personal things like back rubs and favorite meals. Instead of a book of gift certificates, make a three dimensional flower, where each petal is a redeemable coupon. Be creative and sincere in your efforts.

- Written promise to change a negative habit or trait

- Donate time or money to the recipient's favorite charity

- Set up a schedule for relieving someone caring for a sick or elderly relative, say one afternoon or evening a week, or baby-sitting for a harried mom

- Plan an adventure: take your friend or loved one on a picnic or for a ride in the country, or to a movie or play

- Create a memory book or photo album

- Fill a memory jar: write memories of your life/experiences with your parents or special person on slips of paper and put them in a beautiful jar. Have friends and family contribute and give this as a special gift from all of you. This also makes a beautiful expression of sympathy, given to the family of the person who has died.

add a note after the legend—

In keeping with the true essence of giving, I offer you a gift of service (commitment, time). Please accept this with my love and very best wishes.

This gift is my way of saying thank you for all the ways you've given to me over the years.

From me to you, because you're important to my life.

In memory and appreciation of the light and love you have (your loved one has) given to others over the years.

anniversary gifts with meaning

Wedding anniversaries are often known by the element associated with the number of years married: the paper anniversary ... the wooden ... the crystal ... the silver ... the golden ... the diamond. While the origin is uncertain, we do know that the custom of giving gifts appropriate to these themes goes back at least 100 years. Your presents can be serious or whimsical, simple or elaborate, as long as they are heartfelt.

Combine these with some of the legends, such as evergreen, thyme, or rosemary, even if it's only as part of the ribbon or wrapping. Have fun and be creative.

1st:	Paper	13th:	Lace
2nd:	Cotton	14th:	Ivory
3rd:	Leather	15th:	Crystal
4th:	Linen	20th:	China
5th:	Wood	25th:	Silver
6th:	Iron	30th:	Pearl
7th:	Wool	35th:	Coral & Jade
8th:	Bronze	40th:	Ruby
9th:	Pottery	45th:	Sapphire
10th:	Tin	50th:	Gold
11th:	Steel	55th:	Emerald
12th:	Silk	60th:	Diamond

colorful meanings

From the beginning of time, colors have been used in celebration and ceremony, each one symbolizing specific traits or emotions. This list gives you some of the more widely accepted meanings for various colors. Your gifts can range from single candles to symbolically colored clothes, china or jewelry — even a Mercedes, as long as it's the right color for the meaning you want to convey!

Since each color carries several closely-related meanings, choose the most appropriate one and write a short note letting the receiver know just how the color relates to your intentions.

Color	Meaning
White	*protection, peace, healing, truth, purity*
Pink/Rose	*love, harmony, friendship, affection, happiness*
Green	*wealth, fertility, luck, prosperity*
Turquoise	*awareness, creativity, lifts depression*
Purple	*insight, wisdom, dignity, spirituality*
Red	*love, passion, courage, enthusiasm*
Blue	*forgiveness, healing, tranquility*
Apricot	*joy, gentle strength*
Orange	*strength, success, power & authority*
Black	*absorbs and destroys negative energy*
Yellow	*communication, learning, open to new ideas*

herbs & spices

lore, history & meaning

It's often said that the cure for any illness can be found in nature. Throughout history, herbs and spices have been used to maintain physical, psychic and spiritual health. As the New World was being settled, colonial women planted gardens of herbs near the kitchen. Their fragrance and flavor were said to soothe the body and lift the spirit.

Gift of herbs and spices can be used for any occasion. Consider the message you want to convey and choose an herb accordingly. In addition to an actual herb plant for the garden or windowsill, gift ideas might include herbal bath crystals, potpourri, dried flower arrangements and wreaths, jams, jellies, butters, teas or wines.

In addition to the ones listed separately in this book, here are other herbs, their lore and meaning:

ANGELICA: Symbol of angelic love and divine intervention. It is said to have been sent by the angels as a cure for the plague. Medicinally, it is used as a stimulant and expectorant. Angelica can be found in teas, jams and chutneys. Use the hollow part of the stem as a drinking straw for teas and fruit juices.

BASIL: Symbol of both love and hatred. Although basil was sometimes used by the Victorians as a symbol of hatred, it is most commonly used to convey love, comfort the heart, and encourage fidelity. In England and the United States, a single woman would place a pot of basil outside her window to announce her availability.

BAY LEAVES: Symbol of victory and achievement. In ancient times, the Romans and Greeks made a crown of the laurel (bay) leaf for their emperors, poets and scholars as a symbol of victory and honor. The herb's distinctive flavor adds a royal touch to contemporary dishes, particularly soups and stews.

MAY APPLE: Symbol of life and fertility. Biblical lore tells us that Rachel cherished the crushed dried roots of the May apple, claiming they helped women become fertile and bear children. According to legend, this herb was found only where a life had been lost, primarily around the dark side of the gallows. Its profuse growth, despite shade and shadow, symbolizes renewed life and energy.

OREGANO: Symbol of happiness and eternal bliss. According to folklore, anointing yourself with the herb before going to sleep guarantees that you will dream of your future spouse. In ancient times, Greeks planted oregano, also known as wild marjoram, at the grave of their loved ones. If the herb grew strong and healthy, it was a sign that the deceased person was enjoying eternal bliss.

PARSLEY: Symbol of achievement and honor. The Greeks wove parsley into crowns as a sign of "high honors" for the winners of various games. From a practical standpoint, parsley enhances flavor, stimulates digestion and eliminates bad breath. Dill, a member of the parsley family, is said to enhance mental prowess and ward off evil spirits.

PEPPERMINT: Symbol of enchantment. According to ancient scholars, peppermint stimulates the brain, thereby enhancing both charm and intellect. Sprinkling a room with oils of this herb ensures that dinner guests will have a particularly joyful time. Wearing a crown of peppermint leaves while studying enhances intellectual ability.

SAGE: Symbol of eternal youth and virtue. A strong natural preservative, with leaves that are both astringent and antiseptic, sage is regarded as the herb of immortality, ensuring a long and healthy life if ingested regularly. Sage helps memory, aids in digestion, enhances the senses and cleanses the mouth.

plant & flowers

symbols of emotion and virtues

From the very beginning, plants and flowers have been used to symbolize our emotions and the complexity of human relationships — from harmony, jealously and love to issues of life, death and spiritual development. Some believe that flowers and plants are symbols of the virtues permanently inhabited by the soul.

Below are the meanings and superstitions associated with some of the more easily available plants and flowers. For the purpose of gift-giving, don't forget creative interpretations, such as silk varieties, cut flowers, small trees, seeds and even china, pillows, or lap throws emblazoned with the likeness of the plant or flower. And don't forget to write a short personal note relating your gift to the person and the occasion.

APPLE BLOSSOMS:	Hope, awakening
AZALEA:	Temperance, love, romance
BELL FLOWER:	Gratitude
CARNATION:	Love: often used as a symbol of Mother's Day. When sent to a sweetheart, it promises happiness and devotion.
CEDAR:	Thoughtfulness. Also symbolizes steadfastness and unshakable faith.
CHRYSANTHEMUM:	Wealth, abundance, long life
DAISY:	Innocence
GERANIUM:	Faith, friendship
HONEYSUCKLE:	Generosity, devotion, and affection

Giving With Meaning

HYACINTH:	Peace of mind, joy, playfulness
IRIS:	Wisdom & intuition. The Greek word for rainbow, the Iris represents a bridge between heaven and earth.
IVY:	Loyalty
LAUREL:	Glory, ambition
LILY OF VALLEY:	Return to happiness, request for forgiveness
LOTUS/WATER LILY:	Truth (water) and beauty (flower), according to Buddha tradition.
MAGNOLIA:	Power, pride
MARIGOLD:	Jealously
MORNING GLORY:	Affection
OLIVE BRANCH:	Peace
ORANGE TREE:	Generosity
ORCHID:	Beauty, nobility
PETUNIA:	Encouragement, never despair
PANSY:	Thoughtfulness, also a sign of remembrance
PLUM:	Longevity, friendship: It blooms early, lasts many weeks, its sweet nectar satisfies thirst.
RED TULIP:	Passion
SALVIA:	Thinking of you, forever yours
SHAMROCK:	Good luck
WISTERIA:	Welcome
YELLOW JASMINE:	Grace, elegance
ZINNIA:	Thinking of you

stones & gems

birthstone traits & folklore

Folklore tells us that a birthstone influences the wearer's personality by strengthening particular traits. For instance, July babies are given rubies to enhance their contentment; November babies, topaz to emphasize artistic tendencies; and May babies, the emerald, to reflect their natural wisdom and nurturing powers.

Listed here are the twelve birthstones and the traits they have come to symbolize. While they are excellent choices for baby gifts and milestone birthdays, do not feel limited by the months they have come to represent. Give these gemstones based on their specific traits and the recipient's unique needs.

GARNET (JANUARY): Keeps energies flowing; soothes and integrates. Also considered a symbol of friendship and loyalty, it encourages the wearer to become more honest and sincere. *Folklore:* sleeping with a garnet will help a person remember dreams. Will also warn against approaching danger by changing color.

AMETHYST (FEBRUARY): Known as the gemstone of alchemy, the amethyst assists in transforming negative patterns of speech, habits, thoughts and emotions. It protects against overindulgence. *Folklore:* Hold an amethyst beneath your tongue and you can drink any amount of wine without becoming intoxicated.

AQUAMARINE (MARCH): Strong calming influence. Helps soothe and clarify emotions. Known as a purifying and balancing stone, it is recommended for meditation. *Folklore:* This stone will help the wearer become tranquil and "go with the flow."

DIAMOND: (APRIL): Revered for its beauty, brilliance and hardness, this is considered the most powerful of all gems, magnifying the traits of other stones when used in combination. When appreciated for its beauty, rather than material value, the diamond represents fidelity and love and provides the wearer with energy to meet any challenge. *Folklore:* The water into which a diamond has been dipped will cure any illness.

EMERALD (MAY): Known as a heart-healer, the emerald inspires harmony, healing, nurturing, wisdom and patience. This is one of the few stones that enhances the positive traits of every zodiac sign, balancing the wearer's physical, mental and emotional traits. It also bestows the gift of foretelling the future. *Folklore:* Show a serpent your emerald and it instantly becomes blind, protecting you against snake bite. This stone also cures epileptic fits and eye infections.

PEARL (JUNE): Considered magical because of the way it is formed, the pearl and its shell bring protection and good luck. Also associated with heaven and royalty, the pearl symbolizes sacrifice and higher love. *Folklore:* This jewel absorbs all of the wearer's energy patterns. Overly negative energy will eventually "bounce back" to the wearer as a teaching tool for awareness and growth.

RUBY (JULY): Symbolizes passion, courage and a commitment to truth. Helps wearer develop disposition for service and unselfish devotion. *Folklore:* A brilliant, fire-like stone, the ruby actually warms the heart and intensifies positive energies of the circulatory system.

PERIDOT (AUGUST): Honored for its soft glow, this stone is known for its purification aspects. It eases spiritual fears and balances the physical body. A significant tool for releasing emotional burdens and aiding in clairvoyance. *Folklore:* peridot is unique in its cleansing effect on the body, aiding digestion, inflamed bowels and constipation.

SAPPHIRE (SEPTEMBER): Represents hard-earned wisdom and mental stability. Helps the wearer understand the difference between truth and illusion. Aids in discipline and organization. *Folklore:* The sapphire is a significant healing stone, enhancing recovery from illness or injury. Dip the stone in water and then use the water as an eye wash to ward off infection or irritation.

OPAL (OCTOBER): Symbolizes unification and karmic law. Highly absorbent, it picks all of the positive and negative energies emitted into the universe by the wearer and returns them two-fold. Excellent stone for someone who has a positive, helping nature. *Folklore:* The opal's changing color reflects the owner's state of health. Loss of luster means loss of health.

TOPAZ (NOVEMBER): Known as the "golden stone" the topaz intensifies creative energy and mental clarity. Considered to be a stimulant, it is used to promote intuition and abstract thinking and can help individuals coping with trauma or exhaustion. *Folklore:* Wear the topaz to bed for a good night's sleep and to prevent nightmares. Wear it on a headband to speak with spirits.

TURQUOISE (DECEMBER): A magical and highly spiritual stone, symbolizing the mysteries of life. Helps wearer to understand both the physical and spiritual realms of existence. Bestows boldness, courage, and power to succeed. Also provides protection. *Folklore:* Wearing this stone will protect the owner from death by accidents, poison or snakebite.

nature's charms

for luck & protection

Throughout history, men and women have used amulets — ornaments or special pieces of jewelry — to help ensure wealth, luck, love, protection or long life. Here are some natural charms and the meanings behind them.

CAMEO:

Made from the conch shell, it ensures the wearer wealth and good luck. Also serves as a talisman for oratory skills and higher learning.

FOUR LEAF CLOVER:

Classic symbol of good luck. The first leaf to the left of the stem brings fame; the second brings wealth; the third a faithful lover and the fourth good health.

SCARAB :

An insect revered for its ability to decompose matter and create new life, the scarab is an Egyptian symbol of life and vitality. Today, it is most often represented in jewelry, such as in Scarab bracelets and necklaces.

FISH:

Because of its fertility and ability to feed the masses, the fish has traditionally served as a talisman for abundance and prosperity.

PINE CONE:

Associated with Roman and Greek folklore, the pine cone is said to bring health, wealth and power to its owner.

THE CIRCLE:

Round and without end, the circle symbolizes mutual love and affection. From the beginning of time, this simple natural shape has represented the rounding out of life, the essence of pure and total love.

Other universal symbols of luck and protection: rabbit's foot; arrowhead, wishbone, salt, bumble bee, ladybug, beads, coins, and crosses.

Giving With Meaning

gift tags

U se the gift tags on the following pages for the legend appropriate to your gift; on the back, write a short personal note connecting the legend to the gift and the occasion. Use the sample notes in the book as a starting point for your own personal expression.

Acorn - for protection

Because it comes from the mighty oak, the acorn will protect your home when placed on a windowsill during storms.

Bird - conveyor of prayer

According to Native American legend, birds have the power to carry our prayers directly to God with exceptional strength and speed.

Bell - keeper of harmony

According to Irish tradition, the ringing of a bell breaks the spirit of discord and renews the spirit of love.

Garlic - for healing and strength

Throughout history, garlic has been considered a natural healer, capable of improving strength and curing nearly every ailment.

Pineapple - symbol of hospitality

During Colonial times, sea captains returning from the South Seas would bring back a pineapple and spear it on the gate outside his home, to let friends know he was home.

Iron - for healing & protection

Iron - a metal so strong it can be shaped only by fire - is known as the universal weapon against evil spirits, possessing both healing and protective powers.

to:

from:

to:

from:

to:

from:

to:

from:

to:

from:

to:

from:

Evergreen - for eternal hope

According to St. Patrick, green is the color of hope, representing faith, optimism and everlasting life.

Honey & Apples - for a sweet year

Eating apples dipped in honey is a Jewish New Year custom taken from early harvest festivals, symbolizing the promise of a sweet year to come.

Lettuce - for lover's only

Mythology tells us that lettuce is a powerful aphrodisiac, guaranteed to put lovers in just the right mood.

Rosemary - for faithfulness

In ancient times, brides presented each guest with a branch of rosemary, tied with silken ribbons, as a symbol of love and loyalty.

Tomato - for health & wealth

Throughout Italy, tomatoes are a symbol of good fortune. When placed on a mantle, they bring wealth and health into a home.

Turtle - for health & easy pregnancies

According to folklore, turtles are a symbol of patience, good health and long life. They have curative powers and ensure that pregnant women have an easy pregnancy and delivery.

Wedding Basket - destiny fulfilled

In traditional Navajo weddings, a basket made of interwoven coils is used to symbolize the joining of soul mates.

Wheat - symbol of abundance

Throughout history, wheat has symbolized an abundant harvest and used as a wish for fruitfulness.

to:

from:

to:

from:

to:

from:

to:

from:

to:

from:

to:

from:

to:

from:

to:

from:

If you love Giving with Meaning, read the novel that inspired this book. Written by the same author, Field of Destiny is being called a "pager turner, guaranteed to keep you up at night." Giving with Meaning is featured as a book written by the main character, Natalie Marie Davenport, whose destiny is derailed by an impulsive act, thrusting her into a life of secrets, lies and betrayal, where karma and free will collide and a single decision has the power to change everything.

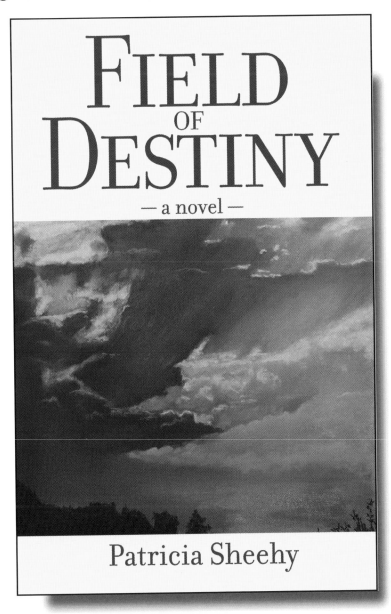

FIELD
OF
DESTINY

— a novel —

Patricia Sheehy

Printed in the United States
80863LV00001B